10/23/01

S0-BXW-622

DISCA

Bible Stories
FROM THE
New Testament

retold by **Meredyth Inman**
illustrated by **Kathy Mitchell**

*With thanks to Reverend Steve LaBaire, St. Luke's Parish, Westborough, Massachusetts,
for his time and expertise in reviewing this book.*

A Random House PICTUREBACK® Book

Random House 🏠 New York

Library of Congress Cataloging-in-Publication Data

Inman, Meredyth. Bible stories from the New Testament / retold by Meredyth Inman ; illustrated by Kathy Mitchell.
p.   cm.   ISBN 0-375-81017-X
1. Bible stories, English—N.T.   [1. Bible stories—N.T.]   I. Mitchell, Kathy (Kathleen Puccio), ill.
BS2401 .I55   2001   225.9'505—dc21   00-037301

Printed in the United States of America January 2001 10 9 8 7 6 5 4 3 2 1

Jesus Is Born

Once there was a young woman named Mary. She lived in the town of Nazareth in the country of Galilee. She was supposed to marry a man named Joseph.

One day, an angel came to see her. "Don't be afraid, Mary!" the angel said. "God will bless you with a son. His name will be Jesus. The child will be the Son of God."

Then the angel visited Joseph and told him to take care of Mary and her baby.

After they were married, Joseph and Mary journeyed to a little town in Judea called Bethlehem. Mary's baby was coming, and they needed to find shelter. But when they got to an inn, the innkeeper said there was no room.

So when Baby Jesus was born, Mary laid Him in a manger, where the animals ate.

Luke 1–2, Matthew 1

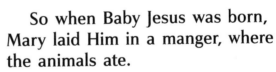

The Journey of the Magi

When Jesus was born, the Magi, a group of wise men from a distant land, saw a bright star in the sky. They knew the star meant the Son of God had been born.

The star led them to the manger where Jesus lay. When they found the baby, they gave Him gifts of gold, frankincense, and myrrh.

Matthew 2

Escape to Egypt

In Judea, there was a king named Herod. He was jealous of Baby Jesus. He heard people whispering that Jesus would be the new king. He ordered his soldiers to search for Baby Jesus and kill Him!

An angel warned Joseph in a dream. So Joseph and Mary took Baby Jesus and escaped to Egypt. When Herod died, they returned to Galilee.

Matthew 2

Jesus in the Temple

When Jesus was twelve, Joseph and Mary took Him to Jerusalem for the festival of Passover. When the celebration was over, they started home. Soon they realized that Jesus was missing. Jesus' parents were worried.

They searched and searched, but no
one could find Him. On the third day, they
went to the temple to pray. There was Jesus,
telling stories to the elders and teachers.
No one could believe the boy's wisdom!

"You have been lost for
three days!" said His parents.
"I am not lost," said Jesus.
"I am in My Father's house!"

Luke 2

Jesus Is Baptized

John the Baptist was a holy man.
He told people that the Son of God
was coming. He baptized believers
in the Jordan River.

One day, Jesus asked John to baptize Him.
John knew that Jesus was the Son of God.
"It is you who should baptize me!" John told
Him.

But Jesus said that God wanted
John to do the baptism. When Jesus was
baptized, a voice from Heaven said, "This
is My son. I am very pleased with Him!"

Matthew 3, Mark 1, Luke 3, John 1

The Twelve Apostles

Jesus had many friends. Some were fishermen. Jesus said God wanted them to be fishers of men. So they left their friends and families to follow Jesus and help teach people about God. They were called apostles, or disciples.

Jesus' Friends

Some of Jesus' friends used to steal and do other bad things.

Jesus told them that God loves everyone. He said that even people who do bad things can try to be good.

God is very happy when a person who was bad decides to be good!

Matthew 4, 9–10, Mark 1–3, Luke 5–6

The Sermon on the Mount

Crowds of people came to listen to Jesus speak. This is what He told them:
Blessed are the gentle, for they will inherit the earth. Blessed are the pure in heart, for they will see God. Blessed are the peacemakers, for they will be called God's children.

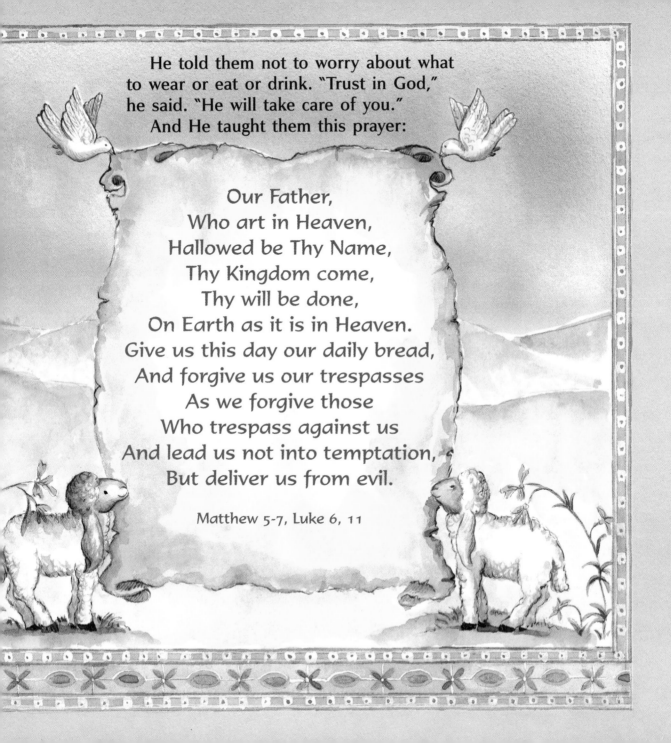

He told them not to worry about what
to wear or eat or drink. "Trust in God,"
he said. "He will take care of you."
And He taught them this prayer:

Our Father,
Who art in Heaven,
Hallowed be Thy Name,
Thy Kingdom come,
Thy will be done,
On Earth as it is in Heaven.
Give us this day our daily bread,
And forgive us our trespasses
As we forgive those
Who trespass against us
And lead us not into temptation,
But deliver us from evil.

Matthew 5-7, Luke 6, 11

The Prodigal Son

Jesus told His disciples this story:
Once a rich man had two sons.
One son took his share of the
family money and left home.
The other stayed with his father.

The son who
left was foolish
and spent his
money on silly
things.

Soon he was poor and had to
beg for food. He returned home
and asked his father if he could
work as his servant.

The father was very happy his son was home and threw a big party. The other son was mad. "I was the loyal son, and you never gave *me* a party," he said.

"Son, I have found your brother again," said the father. "Let's all be happy that he's home."

God is like the father, said Jesus. He is happy when you return to Him.

Luke 15

The Good Samaritan

One day, a lawyer asked Jesus how he could tell if someone was his friend. Jesus told him a story:

Once there was a man traveling alone. A gang of robbers beat him up and stole his money. He was hurt badly.

A priest came along, but he crossed to the other side of the road. He didn't help the poor man.

A Levite, who worked with priests in the temple, also saw the injured man. He didn't stop to help, either.

The third traveler was a Samaritan. Samaritans were enemies of the man's people. But when the Samaritan saw the hurt man, he felt sad. He cleaned the man's cuts and carried him to an inn.

Even though he was supposed to be an enemy, he was really the man's best friend.

Jesus told everyone to be like the good Samaritan.

Luke 10

Jesus Heals Jairus' Daughter

One day, a man named Jairus came to Jesus for help. "My daughter is dying," he cried. "Please make her well."

Jesus went to the man's house. "It's too late," wept her family. "She is already dead."

Then Jesus performed one of his many miracles.

"The little girl is not dead," Jesus told them. "She is only sleeping." He took the child's hand and said, "Little girl, get up from your bed."

The girl opened her eyes and climbed out of bed. It was a miracle!

Matthew 9, Mark 5, Luke 8

Jesus Welcomes the Little Children

One day, a group of little children crowded around Jesus. His disciples tried to push them away, but Jesus stopped his followers.

"Let the children come to Me," He said. "Only those who are open and trusting like little children will go to Heaven." Then Jesus blessed the children.

Matthew 18, 19, Mark 9, 10, Luke 9, 18

Jesus Feeds the Crowd

One day, more than five thousand people came to hear Jesus speak. Jesus told His disciples to feed the crowd.

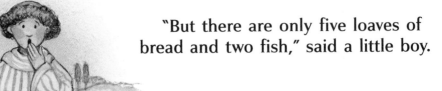

"But there are only five loaves of bread and two fish," said a little boy.

"How can we feed more than five thousand people with so little food?" asked the disciples.

Jesus blessed the bread and fish. Then He told His disciples to pass out the food.

Not only did everyone have enough to eat, but there was food left over! It was another miracle.

Matthew 14, Mark 6, Luke 9, John 6

The Last Supper

Jesus and His disciples ate the Passover meal together.
Jesus knew He would never see His friends again.
He blessed the bread and the wine, and told His friends
to remember Him when they ate it.

"One of you will betray Me," Jesus said.

The disciples were upset. Who could it be?

"It is the one to whom I give this bread," Jesus told them. He broke off the bread and handed it to Judas. "Do what you must," Jesus said to him.

Matthew 26, Mark 14, Luke 22, John 13

Jesus on the Cross

Judas told Jesus' enemies where to find Him. Soldiers came and arrested Jesus. They dressed Him in a purple robe and placed a crown of thorns on His head. They made fun of Him. They hit Him and spat on Him. They made Him carry a heavy cross up a hill. Then they nailed Him to the cross.

"Forgive them, Father," Jesus said.
"They don't know what they're doing."

After Jesus died, His friends buried Him
in a tomb. The entrance was sealed with
a rock.

Matthew 26-27, Mark 14-15, Luke 22-23, John 18-19

Jesus Rises

The next day, one of Jesus' friends went to His tomb. The rock had been rolled away. Jesus' body was gone!

"Jesus has risen from the dead!" said an angel.

Then Jesus appeared to all His friends. "Go into the world," He said, "and tell everyone I am alive and to believe in Me."

Matthew 28, Mark 16, Luke 24, John 20